WORK with ENGLISH

Workbook

Cornelsen

Work with English – Workbook wurde geplant und entwickelt von der Redaktion Moderne Fremdsprachen des Cornelsen Verlages, Berlin.

Verfasser/innen:	Isobel Williams Steve Williams
Projektleitung:	Jim Austin
Verlagsredaktion:	Andreas Goebel
Außenredaktion:	Christine House
Bildredaktion:	Gertha Maly, Jürgen Frey
Layout und technische Umsetzung:	Sylvia Lang, Andrea Päch
Illustrationen:	Uli Österle (S. 10, 18, 58) Oxford Designers & Illustrators
Umschlaggestaltung:	Ellen Meister

www.cornelsen.de

Die Links zu externen Webseiten Dritter, die in diesem Lehrwerk angegeben sind, wurden vor Drucklegung sorgfältig auf ihre Aktualität geprüft. Der Verlag übernimmt keine Gewähr für die Aktualität und den Inhalt dieser Seiten oder solcher, die mit ihnen verlinkt sind.

1. Auflage, 9. Druck 2014

Druck: Stürtz GmbH, Würzburg

ISBN 978-3-464-06276-0

PEFC
PEFC/04-31-1404

PEFC zertifiziert
Dieses Produkt stammt aus nachhaltig bewirtschafteten Wäldern und kontrollierten Quellen.

www.pefc.de

Inhaltsverzeichnis

1 Saying hello

Working with words

1 Family tree

Look at the family tree and complete the sentences with eight of the twelve words in the box.

~~brother~~ • daughter • father • grandfather • grandmother • half-sister • husband • mother • sister • son • step-father • wife

grandfather = Großvater
grandmother = Großmutter
daughter = Tochter
son = Sohn
wife = (Ehe)Frau
husband = (Ehe)Mann

Do you know other 'family' words?

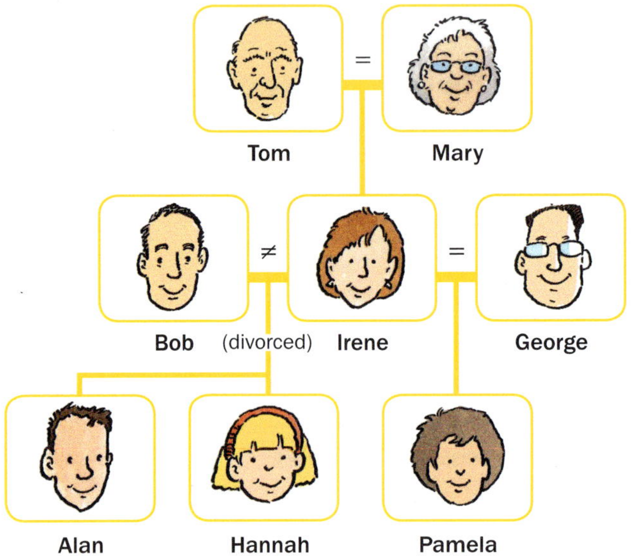

Example: Alan is Hannah's *brother*.

1 Bob is Hannah's ________.
2 Tom is Mary's ________.
3 George is Alan and Hannah's ________.
4 Irene is George's ________.
5 Hannah is Alan's Sister.
6 Mary is Alan and Hannah's grandmother
7 Alan is Irene's son.
8 Pamela is Alan and Hannah's half sister

2 Hobbies

Complete the crossword using the picture clues.

Working with language

3 The simple present

Complete the table with forms of the verb to work. Some of the parts have been done for you.

Aussagen	Verneinungen	Fragen	Kurzantworten
I *work* .	I don't .	Do I work ?	Yes, I do ./No, I don't .
You work .	You don't .	Do you work ?	Yes, you do ./No, you don't.
He works.	He *doesn't work* .	Does he work?	Yes, he does ./No, he doesn't.
She works.	She doesn't .	*Does* she *work* ?	Yes, she does ./No, she doesn't.
It works .	It doesn't .	Does it work ?	Yes, it *does.* /No, it *doesn't* .
We work .	We don't .	Do we work ?	Yes, we do ./No, we don't .
They work.	They don't .	Do they work?	Yes, they do ./No, they don't.

4 Talking about things which happen regularly

a Mary is talking about herself and her family. Cross out the wrong form of the verbs.

Hi! I'm Mary Brown. I *live/ ~~lives~~*[1] in London with my parents, my brother Jacob and my sister Lucy. Lucy and I *doesn't have/ don't have*[2] any pets but Jacob *has/ have*[3] a dog called Sammy. We all *get up/ gets up*[4] at 7.00. Jacob, Lucy and I *leave/ leaves*[5] for school at 8 o'clock. Mum *get/ gets*[6] the bus to work. She usually *leave/ leaves*[7] the house at 8.30. Dad *doesn't work/ don't work*[8]. We *don't have/ doesn't have*[9] the same hobbies. On Tuesday and Thursday I *play/ plays*[10] football. Once a week Mum and Dad *go/ goes*[11] swimming. Jacob *enjoy/ enjoys*[12] cooking and Lucy *like/ likes*[13] ice skating.

b Use the correct form of the verbs in the box to complete the sentences.

cook • do • not enjoy • live • play • not stay • work

1 Mary and her family live in London.
2 Jacob plays with his dog after school.
3 Mary's mum doesn't stay at home. She works in an office.
4 Mary's dad cooks lunch at 12 o'clock.
5 Mary and her mum don't enjoy cooking.
6 Mary, Lucy and Jacob do their homework in the evening.

5 Negatives

Make the following sentences negative. Then give the correct information.

Example: Sally lives in ~~Glasgow~~. (London) *Sally doesn't live in Glasgow. She lives in London.*

1 Jeff goes to school by ~~bus~~. (bike)

____

2 Tim and Madge get up at ~~8.30~~. (7.00)

____

3 Iris leaves the house at ~~9.00~~. (8.30)

____

4 Martin goes to the disco ~~once a week~~. (once a month)

____

5 Don works ~~in an office~~. (at home)

Don doesn't work, he works at home

6 Cathy ~~does aerobics~~ on Monday and Wednesday. (plays tennis)

Cathy doesn't do aerobics, she plays tennis

6 Question words

Complete the questions with the words below. Then match the answers. The first one has been done for you.

Who • ~~When~~ • ~~Where~~ • ~~How often~~ • ~~How~~ • ~~What~~

1 *Where* does Sally live? → e		a She plays tennis.
2 How off does Jeff travel to school?		b Once a month.
When 3 at 7:00 do Tim and Madge get up?		c Pat.
4 How often does Martin go to the disco?		d By bike.
5 What does Cathy do on Monday and Wednesday?		e In London.
6 Who does Andy play football with?		f At 7.00.

Revision

7 The verb to be

x

Use the information about Rocky Starr to complete the FAQ page on his website (see opposite page). Two of the FAQs have already been completed.

Full name:	***Richard Alvin Starr***
From:	Leeds
Age:	22
Colour of eyes:	blue
Height:	1 metre 98
Favourite type of music:	rock
Pet:	dog (Spike)
Job:	rock star

Rocky Starr

Home | News | Info | Events | **FAQ** | Forum | Contact

1	Where are you from?	It's Richard Alvin Starr.
2	↓	Leeds.
3	What's your age?	I'm 22.
4	*What colour are your eyes?*	They're blue.
5	*How tall are you?*	I'm 1 metre 98.
6	What kind of music do you like?	Rock.
7	What your dog's name?	My dog's name is Spike.
8	Who are you? What's your job?	I'm a rock star.

Done | Internet

Writing

8 Writing about yourself

X

Fill in this online dating form with your details. Use your dictionary if necessary.

My full name is Pro	I'm from Ukraine	Age 26	Height 1,62
Colour of eyes are green	My favourite type of music is Hindi		

Write 50–60 words about yourself and your daily routine.

I'm Marta, I go 5 times a week to high school. After school I do something eat than I take a rest and start to learn ~~learning~~ for the school. I often listen to hindi music. In my free time I do go to cinema or for a coffee with my friends

Ich kann ...

Complete the table with things you can do in English.

jemanden nach seinen Hobbys fragen:	*What are your hobbies? Do you like sport?*
Auskunft über mich geben (Hobbys, Herkunft, Haustiere usw.):	*I enjoy* sleeping
	I have a pet
jemanden fragen, wo, wie, wann oder wie oft er / sie etwas macht:	*When do you* go to bed
	How often do you go to gym
sagen, was ich nicht mache:	*I don't* play football
sagen, was ich immer / manchmal / nie mache:	*I sometimes* go swimming
	I never clean my flat

2 Free time

Working with words

1 Free-time activities

a Match the verbs below with the 12 words in the puzzle to make free-time activities. One has been done for you.

b	o	o	k	s	c	d	s	t	f
d	v	d	s	p	o	r	t	e	o
s	w	i	m	m	i	n	g	n	o
p	h	o	t	o	s	w	j	n	t
m	u	s	i	c	l	q	e	i	b
w	v	d	v	i	d	e	o	s	a
m	a	g	a	z	i	n	e	s	l
s	h	o	p	p	i	n	g	z	l

do ____________

go ____________

listen to *cds,* ____________

play ____________

read ____________

take ____________

watch ____________

b Can you think of any more? ____________

2 Places to go and things to do

Complete the dialogue using some of these words and phrases.

action film • cinema • comedy • date • go swimming • going for a drink • pub • Saturday • special • the weekend • what about • what's on • what kind of

A What are you doing at ____________ 1?

B I'm not doing anything ____________ 2.

A How would you like to go to the ____________ 3?

B Good idea. ____________ 4 at the Odeon?

A A ____________ 5 with Julia Roberts. My sister says it's very good.

B OK, great! How about ____________ 6 before the film starts?

A Sure. Do you know a good ____________ 7?

B ____________ 8 'The Place' in Green Street?

A Fine. It's a ____________ 9. See you at 7.

3 Translation

Translate these sentences into English. Tip: Use expressions from exercise 2.

1 Was machst du am Samstag? What are you doing on Saturday?
2 Sollen wir schwimmen gehen? What about swimming?
3 Wie wär's, wenn wir ins Kino gingen? How about cinema?
4 Dann bis sechs! See you at 6 pm.

Working with language

4 The present progressive

Complete the table with forms of the verb to work. Some of the parts have been done for you.

Aussagen	Verneinungen	Fragen	Kurzantworten
I ***am working*** .	I'm not working .	am I working?	Yes, I 'm. / No, I 'm not .
He 's working .	He ***isn't working*** .	is he working?	Yes, he is . / No, he isn't .
We are working .	We aren't working .	are we working?	Yes, we are. / No, we aren't.
You are working .	You aren't working .	are you working?	Yes, you are. / No, you aren't.
They are working .	They aren't .	Are they working?	Yes, they are. / No, they aren't

5 What are they doing?

Use these verbs in the present progressive to complete the sentences.

~~drink~~ • ~~have~~ • meet • ~~play~~ • ~~read~~ • ~~sleep~~ • ~~wait~~ • work

1

2

3

4

5

6

7

8

1 He 's reading a book.
2 She's working in her room.
3 The cat is sleeping.
4 I 'm waiting for the bus.
5 They are drinking coffee.
6 We're having breakfast.
7 Jenny 's playing tennis.
8 Dave is meeting friends.

6 Describing a picture

Look at the picture. Write sentences about Mike and his dogs, Rex and Spike. Use the present progressive.

Examples: (listen to music) Mike*'s listening to music.*

(play in the garden) Rex and Spike *aren't playing in the garden.*

1 (play his guitar) Mike ______

2 (sit on the floor) He ______

3 (watch TV) He isn't watching TV

4 (do his homework) He isn't doing his homework

5 (sleep on the bed) Rex and Spike are sleeping on the bad

6 (fight with other dogs) They aren't fithing with othe dogs

7 Questions

Make questions. Use the present progressive.

Example: you / work / at the moment? *Are you working at the moment?*

1 you / phone your mum? Are you phoning your mom?

2 What / Rob and Tina / cook? What are Rob and tina cooking?

3 Lea / play with her sister? ist Lea plaeyng with her sister?

4 Where / Mandy / go? Where is Mandy going?

5 we / talk too loud? Are we talk too laud?

6 Who / Cathy / sit with? Whom ist Cathy sitting with?

7 Ann and Joe / learn / English? aren Ann and learning Englisch?

8 I / do this right? Am I doing this right?

Revision

8 The simple present

Write sentences and questions using these words.

1 always / do aerobics / on Saturday afternoon / I

I alway do aerobics on Saturday afternoon

2 at the gym / arrive / on time / never / you

You never arrive at the gym on time.

3 at the weekend / always go to the disco / John?

Does John always go to the disco at the weekend?

4 Grace / every evening / phone / me

Grace phones me every evening

Writing

9 Writing about yourself

a Complete the diary pages with things about your typical weekend.

Time of day	Friday	Saturday	Sunday
morning	school		
afternoon	make homwork		
evening	take a rest		

b Now write 50–60 words about your typical weekend.

Ich kann ...

Complete the table with things you can do in English.

sagen, was ich gerade mache:	I'm prepering for a test
fragen, was jemand gerade macht:	What are you doing right now?
jemanden einladen:	Would you like to come to my house?
	How about a movie on Friday?
Einladungen annehmen oder ablehnen:	Thanks, I'll come to you on Friday.
	Sorry, I'm not coming, I'm affraid

3 Other cultures

Working with words

1 Holidays and travelling

Complete the crossword with words to do with holidays and travelling. The first letter of each word has been given.

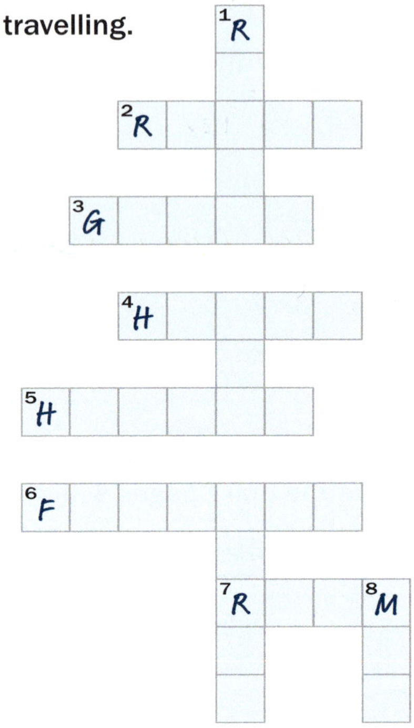

Across
2 You should plan this before you go on a long trip.
3 Someone who tells you about the places you are visiting.
4 A place where you can stay. Sometimes it's expensive.
5 Another place where you can stay. It's usually cheap to stay here.
6 Not at home; not near.
7 A place where you can sleep.

Down
1 A lot of people dream about a trip like this.
8 Something you need so that you don't go the wrong way.

2 Things to do on holiday

Complete this postcard. Use the words in the box.

backpackers' hostel • danced • guide • museum • pub
shopping • tickets • walk

Hi Mike,

Eva and I arrived here in Glasgow last Friday and booked into a 

______ ¹ in the city centre. We went for a  ______ ², then we went to a  ______ ³. Later we went to a club and  ______ ⁴ till about 3 a.m. On Saturday afternoon we went  ______ ⁵. On Saturday night we got 

______ ⁶ for a rock concert. The music was really loud and the atmosphere was brilliant. On Sunday we went to a  ______ ⁷. After that we went on a tour. The  ______ ⁸ told us a lot of interesting things about the city. I'll tell you more about our trip when I see you next week!

Love,

Katie

Working with language

3 The simple past

Complete the table with forms of the verb to work. Some of the parts have been done for you.

Aussagen	Verneinungen	Fragen	Kurzantworten
I *worked* ______.	I ______.	______ I ______?	Yes, I ______. / No, I ______.
She ______.	She ______.	*Did* she *work*?	Yes, she ______. / No, she ______.
We ______.	We ______.	Did we ______?	Yes, we ______. / No, we ______.
You ______.	You ______.	Did you ______?	Yes, you ______. / No, you ______.
They ______.	They ______.	Did they ______?	Yes, they ______. / No, they ______.

4 The simple past of the verb to be

a Complete with was or were.

I was, he/she/it was, you were, we were, they were.

b Complete the sentences with was or were.

1 Gerd and Jo were in India last month.

2 I was in the USA last year.

3 The plane ticket to the USA were very expensive.

4 Kelly was on holiday with her sister two weeks ago.

5 There were a lot of museums in the city they visited.

6 We were at a concert yesterday.

7 Were you on holiday last week?

8 Was the weather good?

5 Questions

Ask questions using the simple past.

Example: you / go on holiday last year? *Did you go on holiday last year?*

1 Where / Tony / go on holiday? Where did Tony go on holiday?

2 Where / you / stay on your last holiday? Where did you stay on your ...?

3 What / you / see at the museum? What did you see at the museum?

4 How much / the trip / cost? How much did the trip cost?

5 When / they / arrive at the hostel? When did they arrive at the hostel?

6 Janice / have a good holiday? Did Janice have a good holiday

7 the hotel / be / expensive? Was the hotel expensive?

8 the rooms / be / comfortable? Were the rooms comfortable?

6 Irregular verbs

a Complete with the simple past of these irregular verbs.

1 be was / were	4 fly floo	7 sleep slept
2 buy bought	5 go went	8 swim swam
3 eat ated	6 have had	9 write wrote

b Use the simple past form of the verbs above to complete the sentences.

1 Keith and Linda *flew* to Ireland last year. The weather ________ lovely.

2 They were camping. They slept in a tent.

3 They usually ate in fast food restaurants when they were in Ireland.

4 Linda weared a bikini and swam in the campsite pool.

5 Keith had a good holiday. He ________ a lot of postcards.

7 Questions and answers

Complete the questions with the correct form of the verbs in brackets. Then match them to Keith's answers.

1 *Did you enjoy* (you / enjoy) your holiday, Keith?
2 Where did ________ (you / go)?
3 Did you ________ (you / stay) in a hotel?
4 Were (be) the Irish countryside nice?
5 Were (be) the Irish people friendly?
6 Did ________ (you / go) to an Irish pub?
7 Did you drink (you / drink) a lot of Guinness?

a No, I don't like beer.
b Yes. We listened to Irish music.
c Yes it's beautiful.
d Yes, I did.
e We went to Donegal.
f Yes, they were.
g No, we didn't. We went camping.

Revision

8 Possessive s or the short form of is?

Add an apostrophe where needed. Say why you have added it – to show a possessive or the short form of is.

Example: This is Keiths rucksack. *This is Keith's rucksack. (possessive)*

1 Hes on holiday at the moment. He's

2 Its nice today. It's

3 Is this the right hotel? Its name is different to the one on the itinerary. It's

4 The guys we met on the trip were very nice. ________

5 Sue's tickets are in the bag. ________

Writing

9 Countries and nationalities

Fill in the name of the country and the nationality of the person in the first column.

	Famous person	Country	Nationality
1	the Queen	Briten	britisch
2	Francesco Totti	Italy	Italien
3	Gérard Depardieu	France	Fransh
4	Mikhail Gorbachev	Russia	Russian
5	Julia Roberts	America	Amerikan

10 Describing your holiday

a Put the words and phrases from the box into the mind map.

cold • expensive • fun • in a hostel • in a hotel • nice • on a boat • on a bus • go shopping • go sightseeing • take a trip • warm • with friends

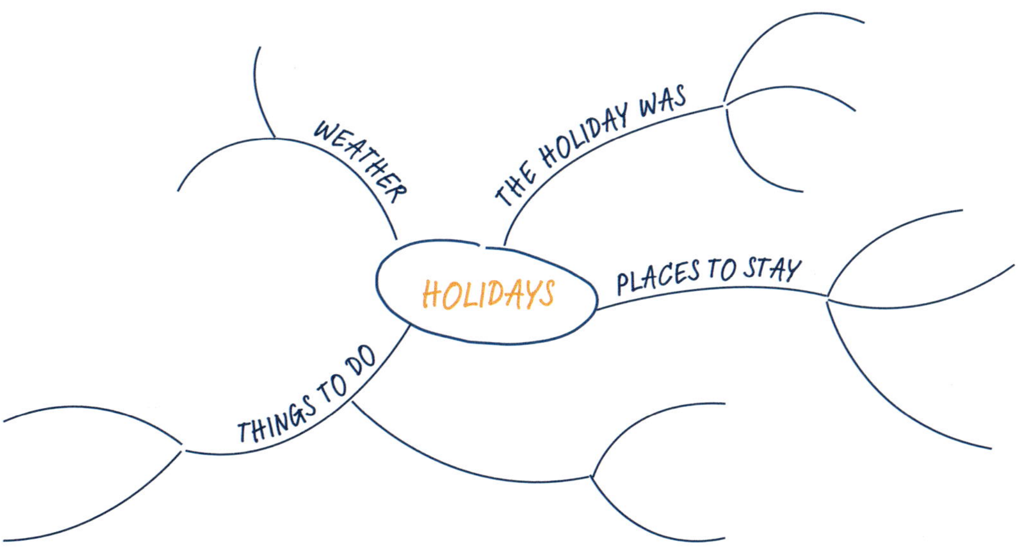

b Use the mind map to write 50–60 words about your last holiday.

____

____

____

Ich kann ...

Complete the table with things you can do in English.

von Erlebnissen berichten: *Last year* __________

nach Urlaubserlebnissen fragen: *Did you* __________

Interesse bekunden: *Really? That* __________

4 Keeping up to date

Working with words

1 Odd one out

Which word doesn't fit? Cross out the wrong word and replace it with another one from the box.

~~belly button ring~~ • ear • eyeliner • grey • ladies • T-shirt

Example:	earring	~~scarf~~	stud	nose ring	belly button ring
1	eyelash	nose	forehead	hand	
2	pink	black	pale	red	
3	false eyelashes	lipstick	piercings	henna	
4	shoes	thin	jeans	jacket	
5	photo	parents	kids	neighbours	

2 Clothes

Find ten items of clothing hidden in the cupboard.

S	P	A	J	A	C	K	E	T
W	U	T	E	S	O	C	K	S
E	L	S	A	A	R	L	I	H
A	L	S	N	N	R	I	L	I
T	O	H	S	C	A	R	F	R
S	V	A	U	R	O	I	S	T
H	E	S	I	I	I	K	H	E
I	R	S	T	O	J	K	O	J
R	J	O	W	H	P	S	E	A
T	R	A	I	N	E	R	S	P

Working with language

3 The going to future

Complete the sentences with going to and the verbs in brackets. Decide what each sentence expresses and tick (✓) the correct box.

	Plans	Something is (not) going to happen soon
1 We're going to invite lots of people to our party next week. (invite)	✓	
2 Why are you wearing your shorts? – I ______ round the park. (run)		
3 That man is driving too fast. He ______ an accident. (have)		
4 I feel terrible. I think I ______. (be sick)		
5 Aidan ______ these jeans. (not buy)		
6 We ______ our friends today. (visit)		
7 It's not very cold. It ______. (not snow)		

4 Questions

Ask questions using going to.

1 When ______ (you / get) a new tattoo?

2 What ______ (you / wear) to the party?

3 How much ______ (she / spend) on her holiday clothes?

4 ______ (you / buy) these shoes?

5 ______ (Jay / get) some more piercings?

5 Comparatives and superlatives

Complete the table with the comparative and superlative forms of the adjectives. Two words have already been filled in.

	Adjective	Comparative	Superlative
Einsilbige Adjektive	hot	hotter	
Zweisilbige Adjektive, die auf -y enden	funny		(the) funniest
Adjektive mit zwei und mehr Silben	beautiful		
Unregelmäßige Adjektive	good bad		

6 Talking about clothes

Choose the correct word from the brackets.

1 Mike is going to wear his ______________ (best / better) clothes for the interview.
2 These are my ________________________ (more comfortable / most comfortable) jeans.
3 This pullover is _________________ (nicer / nicest) than the others.
4 The blue scarf is ___________________ (cheaper / cheapest) than the green one.
5 Is that the ___________________ (larger / largest) size you have?
6 This is the ________________________ (more expensive / most expensive) jacket.

7 Tattoos

Complete Hardy's statement with words from the box.

best • biggest • ~~cool~~ • expensive • good • more interesting • smaller • tougher

'You can get some *cool* [1] body decorations. I think tattoos are a ____________ [2] way to tell people which group you belong to. Some men want to show that they are _________________ [3] than other men and get the ___________________ [4] and most ____________ [5] tattoos they can find. I think ________________ [6] tattoos which make a statement are ______________________ [7]. My tattoo is the ______________ [8] tattoo in the world!'

Revision

8 there is or there are?

Complete these sentences.

Example: *There are* no XL jeans in the shop.

1 ___________________________ a lot of different types of body decorations.
2 ___________________________ any interesting boutiques in your town?
3 ___________________________ a rule at our school: no T-shirts with stupid messages on them.
4 ___________________________ a tattoo you really like?
5 ___________________________ lots of reasons not to pierce your ears yourself.
6 ___________________________ a lot of advertising for expensive clothes.

Writing

9 **In my opinion ...**

a **Read what a British teacher thinks about school uniforms. Circle the four phrases she uses to give her opinion.**

Helen Moore: I think that school uniforms are a good idea. I feel that when everybody wears the same clothes nobody looks different from anybody else. In my opinion, this is better as nobody has to think about fashionable clothes. A uniform shows which school you belong to and, in my view, this also helps people find a group feeling.

b **Do you agree or disagree with Mrs Moore? Make two lists, then write 50–60 words saying what you think. Use some of the phrases you marked in part a.**

good things about school uniforms	bad things about school uniforms
– *everybody is the same*	

Ich kann ...

Complete the table with things you can do in English.

über Pläne und Vorhaben sprechen:	*I'm going to*
Dinge oder Personen vergleichen:	*Tina's tattoo is*
	but Sarah's tattoo
meine Meinung sagen:	*I think tattoos*
	In my opinion,
jemanden nach seiner Meinung fragen:	*What*
zwischen Argumenten abwägen:	*On the one hand,*
	On the other hand,

5 Eating and drinking

Working with words

1 Takeaway puzzle

Olli has just ordered some takeaway food. Here is the message he sent – the numbers show the keys on his mobile. Use your mobile to find out what Olli ordered. Parts of the words are given.

Example:

2 abc | 8 tuv | 7 pqrs | * | 6 mno | 3 def | * | 2 abc | 6 mno | 3 def | 3 def | 3 def | 3 def

c u p   o f   c o f f e e

1

4 ghi | 2 abc | 6 mno | * | 7 pqrs | 4 ghi | 9 wxyz | 9 wxyz | 2 abc

__ a __   __ i __ __ a

2

2 abc | 2 abc | 6 mno | * | 6 mno | 3 def | * | 2 abc | 6 mno | 5 jkl | 3 def

c __ __   __ f   __ o __ __

3

2 abc | 4 ghi | 6 mno | 2 abc | 6 mno | 5 jkl | 2 abc | 8 tuv | 3 def | * | 4 ghi | 2 abc | 3 def   2 abc | 7 pqrs | 3 def | 2 abc | 6 mno

__ __ o __ o __ a __ e   i __ e - __ __ e a __

4

2 abc | 4 ghi | 3 def | 3 def | 7 pqrs | 3 def | 2 abc | 8 tuv | 7 pqrs | 4 ghi | 3 def | 7 pqrs | * | 2 abc | 6 mno | 3 def | * | 2 abc | 4 ghi | 4 ghi | 7 pqrs | 7 pqrs

__ __ e e __ e __ u __ __ e __   a __ __   __ __ i __ __

2 Get fit, Olli!

Complete Olli's 'get fit' poster with words and phrases from the box.

caffeine • energy drinks • habit • homemade • nicotine patch • smoking • sugar • takeaway

Kick the ______________ 1!

Don't drink too many ______________ 2. They are full of ______________ 3 and that makes you nervous. They also contain a lot of ______________ 4 and that's bad for your teeth. Stop ordering meals from the ______________ 5. A ______________ 6 meal is always healthier. Give up ______________ 7. Buy a ______________ 8 today!

Working with language

3 Countable and uncountable nouns

Which of these things are countable? Which of them are uncountable? Make two lists.

a slice of toast • butter • tea • a cup of coffee • a piece of cake • chocolate • sweets • coke • a can of energy drink • bread

Countable: ______________________________

Uncountable: ______________________________

4 Quantifiers

a Choose the correct word in the brackets to complete the rule.

A few wird mit ______________ (zählbaren / nicht zählbaren) Substantiven verwendet.

A little wird mit ______________ (zählbaren / nicht zählbaren) Substantiven verwendet.

b Complete the sentences with a few or a little.

1 He had ______________ pieces of toast for breakfast.

2 She drank ______________ cans of beer last night.

3 I only had ______________ piece of chocolate.

4 There are ______________ soft drinks on the shelf.

5 I like ______________ bit of milk in my tea.

6 Can I have ______________ piece of cake, please?

5 some / any, something / anything, somebody / anybody

Choose the correct words from the brackets to complete this dialogue.

Rob Hi Jess! What are you doing?

Jess I'm looking for ______________ 1 (something / anything) special to cook this evening. I'm having ______________ 2 (some / any) friends round.

Rob That's nice. I wish ______________ 3 (somebody / anybody) would invite me round and cook ______________ 4 (something / anything) for me.

Jess Well, maybe you'll be lucky and ______________ 5 (somebody / anybody) will do that soon.

Rob The problem is, I don't know ______________ 6 (somebody / anybody) who can cook. And I've never cooked ______________ 7 (something / anything) special myself. I don't have ______________ 8 (some / any) talent for that sort of thing.

Jess Poor you. Listen, I have an idea. There are ______________ 9 (some / any) simple cookery books over there. Why don't you look at them?

Rob Oh, OK.

6 Adverbs of manner

Complete the sentences using the correct form of the words in brackets.

Example: It isn't good to eat your food *quickly*. (quick)

1 Liz is a great cook. She cooks ___________. (good)
2 Please read the menu __________________. (careful)
3 Try not to be ___________ for your meal. (late)
4 This wine was very expensive. Please drink it _____________. (slow)
5 She could _______________ lose weight. (easy)

7 In a restaurant

a Who says these phrases – the waiter or the customer? Write w or c in the box.

1 Yes. I'll have a hamburger, please. ☐
2 I'd like to see the menu, please. ☐
3 Would you like chips with it? ☐
4 Would you like anything to drink? ☐
5 Enjoy your meal. ☐
6 No, thanks. I'd rather have a salad. ☐
7 Can I take your order now? ☐
8 Some beer, please. ☐

b Make the sentences above into a dialogue.

Customer: *I'd like to see the menu, please.*

...

Waiter: ______________________________
Customer: ______________________________
Waiter: ______________________________
Customer: ______________________________
Waiter: ______________________________
Customer: ______________________________

...

Waiter: ______________________________

Revision

8 much or many?

Choose much or many. Cross out the wrong word.

1 How ~~much~~ / many cans of coke have you drunk today?
2 How much / many is the pizza?
3 Do you know much / many people who don't eat meat?
4 There aren't much / many good restaurants in this town.
5 How much / many times have you tried to lose weight?
6 How much / many caffeine is there in a cup of coffee?

Writing

9 A good restaurant

a Read about The Big German Restaurant, then complete the card on the right with details about a good restaurant you know.

The
Big German Restaurant

24 Happy Street
Phone: 0131/96745

There's a large selection of meals starting at £ **2.50**

German food. Vegetarian meals.

Saturday Special:
All you can eat for £ **10.50**

German beer.

Happy hour: 6 – 8 p.m.
Monday – Friday; all day Saturday.

► The best restaurant in Happy Town. ◄

____

____

The best restaurant in __________ !

There's a large selection of __________

starting at __________ .

__________ food.

Saturday Special:

____________________ .

Happy hour:

____________________ .

Drinks: __________

Phone: __________

b Now write 50–60 words about your favourite restaurant.

____

____

____

____

____

Ich kann ...

Complete the table with things you can do in English.

sagen, wie jemand etwas macht:	*He drives*
	She speaks Spanish very
etwas zum Essen bestellen:	*I'd like*
etwas zum Trinken bestellen:	*I'll*
fragen, wie viel etwas kostet:	*How*
unbestimmte Mengen ausdrücken:	*Would you like* ______ *sugar?*
kleine Mengen beschreiben:	*Yesterday evening I drank*

6 Jobs and training

Working with words

1 Crossword: words about school

Complete the crossword using these clues. The first letter of each word has been given

1 This helps you get a job.
2 People who go to school.
3 The final mark when you do an exam.
4 Something you should never stop doing.
5 The place where you study.
6 When British kids are 12 years old, they go to a ... school.
7 A piece of paper which shows what you have learned.
8 A bookkeeping ... can last two years.
9 Everybody hates doing this.
10 British kids go to a ... school till they are 11.

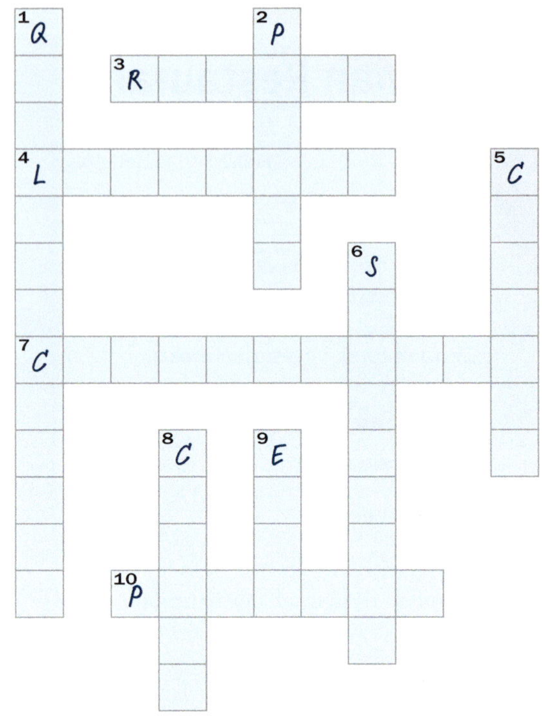

2 Things you learn at college

a Match the English words and phrases to their German translations.

1 foreign language correspondent
2 commercial correspondence
3 translations
4 day release class
5 business letters
6 counting
7 training
8 bookkeeping

a Geschäftsbriefe
b Buchhaltung
c Rechnen
d freier Tag (zur Fortbildung)
e Ausbildung
f Geschäftskorrespondenz
g Fremdsprachenkorrespondent/in
h Übersetzungen

b Complete the text with the English words and phrases above.

Angie didn't want to be unemployed when she left school so she took a job in the ______________[1] department of a big firm. She doesn't like it much. She has never liked maths and she doesn't like ______________[2]. She prefers languages so when her boss asked her if she would like to go back to school, she said yes. 'I'm training to be a ______________[3],' she says. 'I go to a ______________[4] once a week and learn how to write ______________[5] in English and French. I enjoy the ______________[6] classes a lot. I love doing ______________[7].' Angie is happy. 'I'm so pleased to have the chance to do this extra ______________[8],' she says.

Working with language

3 The present perfect

Complete the table with forms of the verb to finish. Some of the parts have been done for you.

Aussagen	Verneinungen	Fragen	Kurzantworten
I *have finished.*	I ______ ______.	______ I ______?	Yes, I ______./ No, I ______.
He ______ ______.	He *hasn't finished.*	______ he ______?	Yes, he ______./ No, he ______.
We ______ ______.	We ______ ______.	______ we ______?	Yes, we ______./ No, we ______.
You ______ ______.	You ______ ______.	______ you ______?	Yes, you ______./ No, you ______.
They ______ ______.	They ______ ______.	______ they ______?	Yes, they ______./ No, they ______.

4 Yes / No answers

Give short answers.

1 Has he done his homework? – Yes, he ______.

2 Have you applied for a job? – Yes, I ______.

3 Has the teacher given out the results? – No, he ______.

4 Have the pupils been busy? – No, they ______.

5 Has Ivan got good marks? – No, he ______.

6 Has the teacher given us too much homework again? – Yes, he ______.

5 What has (not) happened?

Use the words in brackets and the present perfect to explain what has (not) happened.

Example: My bicycle is missing. (someone / steal my bicycle) *Someone has stolen my bicycle.*

1 The classroom is empty. (the pupils / go for lunch) ______

2 I can't find my English book. (I / leave it at home) ______

3 Harry's not going to Lucy's party. (she / not invite him) ______

4 Sarah is going for an interview. (she / buy some new clothes) ______

______

5 There's a test tomorrow and Joe is worried. (he / not look at his books for ages) ______

______

6 We aren't ready to go out. (we / not have lunch yet) ______

6 since or for?

a Complete the rule.

________ steht mit einer Zeitspanne, die angibt, wie lange etwas bereits andauert.

________ steht mit einem Zeitpunkt, an dem etwas begonnen hat.

b Which words and phrases go with since and which with for?

2006 • 5 o'clock • ages • a long time • a month • Christmas • my birthday • Saturday • ten minutes • three days

Since ____

For ____

c Complete the sentences with since or for.

1 Francis and Ivan have known each other ________ they were at school.

2 How long has she worked at JayPegs? – ________ May.

3 I haven't been to the office ________ ages.

4 Anne has been a qualified programmer ________ six months.

5 How long have you had a dictionary? – ________ two weeks.

6 He has been with the boss ________ 9 o'clock this morning.

d Translate the sentences above into German.

1 ____

2 ____

3 ____

4 ____

5 ____

6 ____

7 The simple past or present perfect?

Complete with the correct form of the verbs in brackets. Tip: circle the signal words.

Example: (How long) *have you been* on this course now? (be)

1 I ________ my exams last year. (pass)

2 Kevin ________ any job interviews for ages. (not have)

3 We ________ 40 people yesterday. (interview)

4 Liam ________ an interesting job advertisement in the paper on Saturday. (see)

5 They ________ lots of jobs since they left school. (apply for)

6 ________ the job last week? (get)

Revision

8 a or an?

Complete the sentences with a or an.

I have _____ [1] friend, Sue, who has been unemployed for over a year. Last month _____ [2] English teacher gave Sue _____ [3] good tip. She said, 'When you apply for _____ [4] job and you fill in _____ [5] application form, don't write "unemployed". It gives _____ [6] bad impression.' Sue took the teacher's advice and she's already had _____ [7] interview at one firm. I'm sure she'll find _____ [8] interesting job soon.

Writing

9 My training

The time-line below was made by Jenny T. on 11 April this year. It starts with the year she went to vocational college and shows what she has done since then.

20..	20..	January this year	February	March	2 April	10 April
start college, join economics class	go to Spanish class	do course on Excel/ spreadsheets	buy dictionary		do maths test – passed?	do book-keeping test – passed?

a **Now make your own time-line. Start with the year you went to vocational college and finish with today's date. Add the important things you have done.**

b **Use your time-line to write about what you have done and learned at college. Here is the start of Jenny's text. Notice that she uses both the simple past and the present perfect.**

I started at vocational college in 20... I have been in the economics class for two years.

____

____

____

Ich kann ...

Complete the table with things you can do in English.

jemanden fragen, ob er/sie etwas schon gemacht hat:	*Have you* ______
sagen, dass ich etwas schon mal gemacht habe:	*I've* ______
jemanden fragen, wie lange er/sie etwas schon macht:	*How long* ______
sagen, wie lange ich etwas schon mache:	*I've* ______
sagen, seit wann ich etwas schon mache:	*I've* ______

7 That's life (or is it?)

Working with words

1 Opposites

a What are the opposites of these words? The first one has been done for you.

1	happy	unhappy	5	agree	
2	good		6	fat	
3	fair		7	like	
4	young		8	realistic	

b Complete the sentences with the words from the box above.

1 The result is ______________. The other team played better.
2 He only eats fruit. That's why he's so ______________.
3 She was very ______________ when her boyfriend kissed her sister.
4 I don't ______________ meat but I prefer salad.
5 I don't believe some of his stories. They are very ______________.
6 My grandma is 62 but she doesn't look very ______________.
7 They stole money from an old lady. They are very ______________ people.
8 The brothers often fight. They ______________ about everything.

2 TV programmes

Unscramble the letters to find types of TV programmes.

paso arepo

____

mage whos

____

youcamtrend

____

swen datobarsc

____

tevtedice troys

____

torpss mepgorarm

____

Working with language

3 Modal verbs

Complete the table. Some of the parts have been done for you.

German	English
können	, could , be able to
müssen	must ,
dürfen	
nicht dürfen	
könnte/n	, ,
sollen / nicht sollen, sollte/n	,

4 can/can't, could/couldn't, be able to

Choose the correct form to complete the sentences. Cross out the wrong forms.

1 My driver *was able to / can / couldn't* pick you up at the airport tomorrow.
2 After the operation next week he *won't be able to / couldn't / can't* walk.
3 The boss *can't / is able to / couldn't* see you at the moment. He's busy.
4 He *can / is able to / could* do anything he wanted to when he was a child.
5 I was ill on Saturday so I *can't / wasn't able to / could* go to the party.
6 If things go well, you *are able to / will be able to / were able to* go home tomorrow.
7 It was great on holiday. I *can / was able to / am able to* sleep till lunchtime.
8 Josy got the job in Spain. She *can / is able to / could* speak to the interviewer in perfect Spanish.

5 should or shouldn't?

Write sentences with should or shouldn't and one of the suggestions in the box. The first one has been done for you.

~~buy so many clothes~~ • do it • eat so much • keep quiet sometimes • live together • phone home and say hello • try go to bed before 10 • write a soap opera

1 We never have any money. We shouldn't buy so many clothes.
2 She hasn't seen her family for months. She ______.
3 You have a very interesting life. You ______.
4 He doesn't love her and she doesn't love him. They ______.
5 I'm always tired. I ______.
6 Smoking is expensive. You know you ______.
7 You talk too much. You ______.
8 You're too fat. You ______.

6 don't/doesn't have to or mustn't?

Complete the sentences using don't/doesn't have to or mustn't.

1 The bus leaves at 8 o'clock. We ____________ miss it.

2 It's going to be warm today. You ____________ wear a pullover.

3 You ____________ talk in the cinema. It annoys other people.

4 It's a holiday tomorrow. My dad ____________ go to work.

5 You ____________ buy a dictionary. You can use this one.

6 It's a secret. You ____________ tell anyone else.

7 More modals

Complete the answers with the correct modal verbs.

can't • couldn't • didn't have to • had to • must • needn't • not allowed to • shouldn't

1 How long can I stay? – You ____________ leave before my parents get home.

2 Is the film very scary? – Yes, it is. You ____________ watch it.

3 Where were you yesterday afternoon? – I ____________ go shopping.

4 Was yesterday a holiday? – Yes, Sam ____________ go to school.

5 Did Sarah enjoy her holiday in France? – Not really. She ____________ speak French.

6 What time does the plane go tomorrow? – 12 o'clock. We ____________ get up early.

7 Why did they walk home? – They ____________ get a taxi.

8 Would you like a beer? – No, thanks. I'm ____________ drink alcohol.

8 Describing pictures

Make sentences to match the signs and pictures.

1

2

3

4

5

6

1 Nobody	have to	buy a ticket.
2 Dogs	needn't	smoke here.
3 We	can	switch off our mobiles.
4 People	is allowed to	relax here.
5 He	mustn't	come in here.
6 Old people	can't	swim here.

Revision

9 going to

Complete each dialogue with going to and one of the phrases in the box.

have some soup • hire a car • move there next month • phone him • watch TV

1 A: Have you spoken to Andy lately?

B: No, I haven't. I ______________________________ this evening.

2 A: What are your holiday plans?

B: We ______________________________ and drive to Italy.

3 A: Are you hungry?

B: Yes, I am. I ______________________________.

4 A: Do you have any plans for this afternoon?

B: Yes, we ______________________________.

5 A: Did Yvonne get the job in New York?

B: Yes, she did. She ______________________________.

Writing

10 TV programmes I watched yesterday

a Make notes about what you watched on TV yesterday. What was interesting / boring? Say why.

Name of programme	Type of programme	What happened	My opinion	Reason

b Use your notes to write 60–80 words.

____

____

____

____

Ich kann ...

Complete the table with things you can do in English.

sagen, was ich kann: I can ______________________________

ausdrücken, dass etwas verboten ist: You ______________________________

jemandem einen Rat geben: You ______________________________

sagen, dass ich etwas nicht machen muss: I ______________________________

sagen, dass ich etwas vielleicht machen werde: I ______________________________

8 The right job

Working with words

1 Applying for a job

a Match the English and the German expressions.

1 CV	a Firma
2 prepare	b ankommen
3 job advertisement	c Bewerbungsschreiben
4 company	d Lebenslauf
5 letter of application	e Stellenanzeige
6 find out	f Gesprächspartner/in beim Vorstellungsgespräch
7 interview	g Kandidat/in
8 arrive	h (sich) vorbereiten
9 candidate	i herausfinden
10 interviewer	j Vorstellungsgespräch

b Now use some of the expressions to complete the diagram.

Step 1 Read the ______ ______ carefully. →

Step 2 Use the internet to ______ ______ all about the company. →

Step 3 Write a ______ ______. →

Step 4 Check your ______ to make sure it is correct. →

Step 5 Send your letter and CV to the ______. →

Step 6 Dress smartly for the ______. →

Step 7 ______ at the interview on time. →

Step 8 Smile when you meet the ______. →

Step 9 Get the job!

2 Good and bad candidates

There are ten adjectives in the word square on the next page. First circle the words and then put each adjective into the correct list.

A good candidate is ...	A bad candidate is ...
friendly	______
______	______
______	______
______	______
______	______

L	C	U	D	L	A	T	E	F
A	O	N	I	Z	P	O	I	R
Z	N	E	R	V	O	U	S	I
Y	F	L	T	A	L	M	M	E
D	I	O	Y	N	I	E	A	N
Y	D	P	H	I	T	S	R	D
A	E	Q	T	R	E	F	T	L
U	N	T	I	D	Y	I	O	Y
L	T	C	L	E	A	N	U	S

Working with language

3 Relative pronouns

Cross out the pronouns which are incorrect.

Example: Tell me about the job ~~*who*~~ / *which* / *that* you applied for.

1 Are these the clothes *who* / *which* / *that* you bought on Saturday?
2 That's the teacher *who* / *which* / *that* told me about the job.
3 This is the test *who* / *which* / *that* I had to do in my interview.
4 Can you remember any of the questions *who* / *which* / *that* the interviewer asked?
5 Would you like to see the letter *who* / *which* / *that* I sent?
6 The person *who* / *which* / *that* interviewed me was very friendly.

4 How do you say it in German?

Translate these sentences into German. Remember to add the relative pronouns in German.

Example: Is this the advertisement you saw?

Ist das die Anzeige, die Sie gesehen haben?

1 Think about questions they may ask.

____

2 Have you met the people you're going to work with?

____

3 Here's the shirt I bought for the interview.

____

4 Please tell us about the course you are doing at college.

____

5 Explaining words

A British student wants to know about training in Germany. Explain the German words to him.

Example: What's a *berufliche Schule*? (school / teaches / vocational subjects)

A 'berufliche Schule' is a school which/that teaches vocational subjects.

1 What's an *Azubi*? (person / learning / do a job)

____

2 What's a *Pflichtfach*? (subject / students / have to study)

____

3 What's a *Praktikant/in*? (person / doing / work experience)

____

4 What's an *Abschlussprüfung*? (exam / students / do / end of the course)

____

Revision

6 The simple past

Use verbs in the simple past to complete Ben's story.

I *went*[1] (go) to secondary school in Birmingham. I __________[2] (not like) school, so I __________[3] (leave) at 16. I __________[4] (not do) any vocational training – I __________[5] (want) to get a real job. So I __________[6] (start) work in a factory which __________[7] (make) mobile phones. After a few months I __________[8] (see) that it __________[9] (be) a mistake: the work __________[10] (not be) interesting and I __________[11] (need) more job satisfaction. I __________[12] (apply) for a place at vocational college. Now I'm training to be an electrician.

7 some / any, something / anything

Complete the dialogue about Jackie's interview with some, any, something or anything.

Jackie OK, Mum, I'm going now. Wish me luck!

Mum But you haven't had __________[1] breakfast! You must have __________[2] to eat ...

Jackie No, Mum – really, I can't eat __________[3]. I'm too nervous!

Mum I'll just make you __________[4] sandwiches ...

Jackie Forget it – there isn't time! I have to go now. I'll get __________[5] at the shop.

Mum OK, OK. Good luck!

Jackie Thanks ... Oh, no! I haven't got __________[6] money for the bus. Can you lend me __________[7] money, please?

Mum Of course. Here's ten pounds. Don't be late!

Writing

8 Applying for a job at a workcamp

Complete the application form. Use full sentences where possible.

Application Form: Volunteers International

Name: ______________________

1 When did you leave secondary school?

____

2 What are you doing now?

____

3 Describe any work experience you have had.

____

4 What sort of voluntary work do you want to do?
(e.g. with children / old people, inside/outside, with your hands / a computer)

____

____

5 What languages do you speak?

____

6 Do you have any other useful skills or qualifications?
(e.g. computer skills, driving licence)

____

7 What are you going to do when you leave college?

____

Ich kann ...

Complete the table with things you can do in English.

Personen näher beschreiben:	*This is the man who*
Dinge näher beschreiben:	*This is the car*
einen Begriff umschreiben:	*A mechanic is*
	A
jemanden um Rat fragen:	*What should*
in einem Brief die passenden Anrede- und Schlussformeln anwenden:	*Dear*
	Yours

9 Destination NZ

Working with words

1 Holiday activities

Mike is on an adventure sports holiday in New Zealand. He has sent an email home, but a virus has mixed up some words. Work out the words and complete the programme of events.

We're having a fantastic time in New Zealand.
On Monday there was a 'welcome' reebcuba at the hostel – we got to know lots of people. On Tuesday we did a ubyng pumj – scary, but fun! On Wednesday we went nutminao nikbig in the mountains – hard work! On Thursday we were so tired, we didn't want to do anything – we just decided to lilch uto. Today we went to the habec and played volleyball. Tomorrow we're going poshpnig to buy some souvenirs.

See you soon!
Mike :D

NZ Adventure Holidays – Programme of events

Monday: Make new friends at the *barbecue*.
Tuesday: Do a 40-metre ______.
Wednesday: Go ______
Thursday: Relax and ______ at the hostel.
Friday: Play volleyball on the ______.
Saturday: Go ______ in Auckland.

2 Word families

a Complete the table. Use a dictionary if necessary.

verb	noun	adjective
choose	______	–
______	flight	–
enjoy	______	*enjoyable*
______	invitation	______
live	______	______
plan	______	–

b Now complete the sentences with words from the table on page 36.

1 The sea looks so ______________! I can't wait to have a swim!

2 There are two ______________ tomorrow: hang-gliding or bungy jumping.

3 Are you going to ______________ to Paris or take the train?

4 Have you ______________ your big trip yet?

5 ______________ in New Zealand must be great!

6 Auckland is a very ______________ city – there's always so much to do.

Working with language

3 Talking about the future

Match the situations (a–f) to the tenses (A–D), then find an example (1–6) for each situation.

	a Vorhersagen	1 Our flight takes off at 14.30.
A *going to* future	b feste Pläne mit Zeitangaben	2 I'm sure you'll have a great time in Thailand.
B *will* future	c Fahrpläne und Programme	3 I've just had a good idea – I'll come with you!
C present progressive	d Pläne und Absichten	4 I'll drive you to the airport, if you like.
D simple present	e spontane Entscheidungen	5 Chloe and Sue are going to book a round-the-world trip.
	f Versprechen und Angebote	6 So, we're leaving on the 18th, is that right?

4 Negatives

Make the following sentences negative. Then give the correct information.

Example: The weather will be ~~awful~~ in Ireland. (great)

The weather won't be awful in Ireland. It will be great.

1 The train arrives at ~~half past six~~. (half past seven)

____

2 We're flying to ~~Greece~~ in the summer holidays. (Croatia)

____

3 I'm going to ~~start work~~ as soon as I leave college. (see the world first)

____

4 The food will be ~~horrible~~ in India. (really nice)

____

5 Holiday plans

Complete the dialogue with appropriate future forms of the verbs in brackets.

Josh: When ____________ [1] (you / go) to New Zealand?

Lexi: We ____________ [2] (leave) at 11.30 in the morning, but I have to be at the airport by nine.

Josh: It ____________ [3] (be) very cold in New Zealand, I suppose ...

Lexi: It ____________ [4] (not be) cold at all! It's summer in New Zealand now.

Josh: Oh, right. What ____________ [5] (you / do) when you get there?

Lexi: We ____________ [6] (travel) around and see as much as we can.

Josh: Sounds wicked! I'm sure you ____________ [7] (have) a great time.

Lexi: I hope so. I ____________ [8] (send) you an email when I get there.

Revision

6 The simple present

Translate the questions, then answer them in full sentences. Use short answers if appropriate.

http//www.i-chat-forum.nz

Google

Apple .Mac Amazon eBay Yahoo! News ▾

iChat Forum **Member Profile: kezzi**

real name:	Kylie Thompson
city:	Auckland, NZ
family:	parents Jim and Kathy (divorced); no brothers/sisters
music:	garage, R&B
pets:	2 dogs
interests:	adventure sports, travel
job:	nursery nurse

Example: Hat Kylie Geschwister?

Does Kylie have any brothers and sisters? No, she doesn't.

1 Sind ihre Eltern geschieden? ____________

2 Wohnt sie in Deutschland? ____________

____

3 Hat sie Haustiere? ____________

4 Welche Hobbys hat sie? ____________

5 Was für Musik mag sie? ____________

6 Ist sie Kinderpflegerin? ____________

Writing

7 Holiday competition

a Read the advert below and find out how you can win an adventure holiday.

Celtic Surf Adventure

Win a fantastic three-day adventure on the West Coast of Ireland!

Choose three of these activities:

- bungy jump
- hang-gliding lesson
- mountain bike tour
- whitewater rafting
- boat trip and swim with dolphins.

Write 60–80 words and tell us what you would like to do and why.

• • • • • Send your answer to

b Complete the table with the three activities from the advert you are interested in.

Activity	Reason

c Now write your answer. Use some of the expressions from the box.

I've always wanted to ... • I'd like to ... • I'm (not) going to ... • I love/enjoy ...ing. • I think it will be scary/exciting/fun. • I want to try something different/special. • I'm scared of ...

Ich kann ...

Complete the table with things you can do in English.

in einem Gespräch Überraschung ausdrücken:

Mitgefühl ausdrücken:

jemandem ein spontanes Angebot machen: I

jemandem etwas versprechen: I promise I

eine Fahrplanauskunft geben: The train

10 Keep in touch

Working with words

1 Phone language

Find the words to complete these expressions.

1 *ring* tone
2 text ______
3 internet ______
4 ______ phone
5 monthly ______
6 phone ______

C	A	L	L	G	A	D
M	E	S	S	A	G	E
O	G	R	A	C	T	O
B	B	O	O	C	R	V
I	U	F	E	E	I	L
L	T	E	A	S	N	S
E	M	I	N	S	G	Y

2 Messages

Complete the sentences with verbs from the box. You may need to change the form of the verbs. There are three verbs too many.

answer • download • leave • listen • pay for • receive • ring • suit • ~~talk to~~ • turn off

Example:

No monthly fees – only ______ the calls you make!

1

2

Choose the phone tariff which ______ you best!

3

Click here to ______ our new song.

4

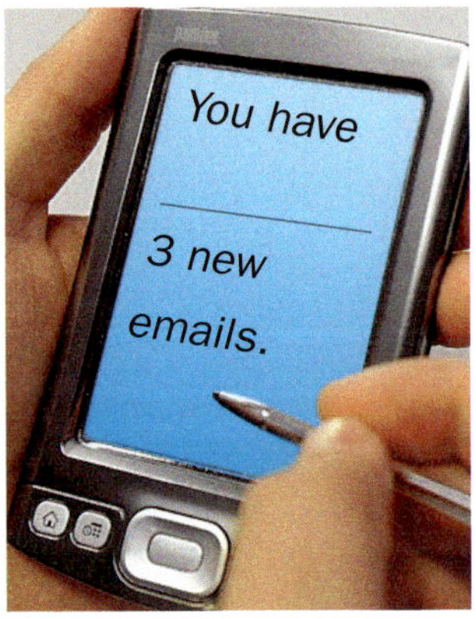

5

6

Working with language

3 Conditional sentences

Cross out the incorrect verb forms.

1 If you *leave* / ~~*will leave*~~ your phone on the bus, you'll be sorry.

2 *I'm not* / I *won't be* disappointed if Ethan doesn't call me tonight.

3 If Paul *won't start* / *doesn't start* soon, he won't finish his homework in time.

4 If you *watch* / *will watch* too many soaps, you turn / will turn into a soap junkie.

5 What *do you do* / *will you do* if you *lose* / *will lose* your job?

6 *I am* / *I'll be* very surprised if Chuck *gets* / *will get* a date with Alison.

4 Saying what will happen

Complete the sentences.

Example: If Nina gets a tattoo, *her mum will go mad*. (her mum / go mad)

1 If you forget your password, ______________________________. (computer / not work)

2 If he drinks too many energy drinks, ______________________________. (feel dizzy)

3 Martin will get a good job ______________________________. (pass his exams)

4 If I go out with you, ______________________________. (my friends / laugh at me)

5 You won't pass the test ______________________________. (not concentrate)

6 If he doesn't answer his phone, ______________________________. (I / not leave a message)

5 Translation

Translate the sentences into English, using the words in brackets.

Example: Wenn Dave heute Abend Zeit hat, ruft er vorher an.

(have time / this evening / phone) *If Dave has time this evening, he'll phone.*

1 Wenn Carol Ski fahren geht, macht sie wahrscheinlich einen Unfall.
(go skiing / probably / have an accident)

____

2 Wenn du ihren Geburtstag vergisst, wird sie traurig sein.
(forget / birthday / be sad)

____

3 Wenn du keinen Internetzugang brauchst, bekommst du einen billigeren Handytarif.
(not need / internet access / get / cheaper / mobile phone tariff)

____

4 Wenn wir uns nicht beeilen, kommen wir zu spät.
(not hurry / be late)

____

6 if or when?

Complete the sentences with if or when.

1 Jake is always busy ________ I call him.

2 ________ Tara wears nose jewellery at work, her boss will be angry.

3 You'll be tired in the morning ________ you go out clubbing tonight.

4 ________ I go to bed at night, I often forget to turn my phone off.

5 ________ Shaun doesn't call us by six, we'll call him.

6 Saskia will be really annoyed ________ she misses *Gute Zeiten, schlechte Zeiten.*

Revision

7 Comparatives and superlatives

Use the table to make comparisons.

File Edit View Favorites Tools Help

Back Forward Stop Refresh Home Search Favorites History Mail Print Edit Discuss

Address http://www.ez-mobile.com/ Links

EZ mobile

Compare any three mobiles here!

		Nokia Z80	Motorola A3i	O2 SmartPhone
1	light	*	**	***
2	useful functions	**	***	*
3	good sound quality	***	**	*
4	big screen	**	*	***
5	looks cool	**	*	***
6	easy to use	***	**	*

Done Internet

1 The O2 SmartPhone is the *lightest* phone.

2 The Motorola A3i has the ________ functions.

3 The Nokia Z80 has the ________ sound quality.

4 The O2 SmartPhone has a ________ screen than the other phones.

5 The Nokia Z80 looks ________ than the Motorola A3i but it doesn't look ________ the O2 SmartPhone.

6 The Motorola A3i is ________ to use than the O2 SmartPhone but the Nokia Z80 is the ________ phone to use.

Writing

8 Mobile phone habits

a Complete the questionnaire.

1 How often do you use these things to keep in touch with friends?
(1 = every day, 2 = often, 3 = sometimes, 4 = rarely or never)

☐ phone calls ☐ emails ☐ text messages ☐ letters

2 How many text messages have you received in the last 24 hours?

☐ none ☐ fewer than 10 ☐ 10–20 ☐ more than 20

3 Which of these features does your mobile phone have?

☐ camera ☐ video camera ☐ internet access ☐ TV ☐ games

☐ other: ____________________

☐ I don't have a mobile phone.

4 How much did your mobile cost? ____________________

5 How do you pay for your calls?

☐ I'm on pay as you go. ☐ I pay a monthly fee. ☐ My parents pay.

6 How much did you spend on phone calls last month? ____________________

7 How important will these things be when you buy your next mobile phone?
(1 = most important, 4 = least important)

☐ low price ☐ lots of functions ☐ small size ☐ good phone plan

b Use your answers to the questionnaire to write about your mobile phone habits. (80–100 words)

____

____

____

____

Ich kann ...

Complete the table with things you can do in English.

im Geschäft sagen, was ich möchte:	*I'd like to*
einen Kunden fragen, ob ich helfen kann:	*Can*
Bedingungen und Folgen formulieren:	*If you send*
sagen, was ich mit meinem Handy machen kann:	*I can*

11 Fame and fortune

Working with words

1 Showbiz vocabulary

Complete the diagram by writing each word or phrase in the correct circle.

~~actor~~ • audience • audition • ~~celebrity~~ • director • extra • get one's big break • gig • gossip • line-up • ~~musician~~ • play a leading role • play the drums • recording • script

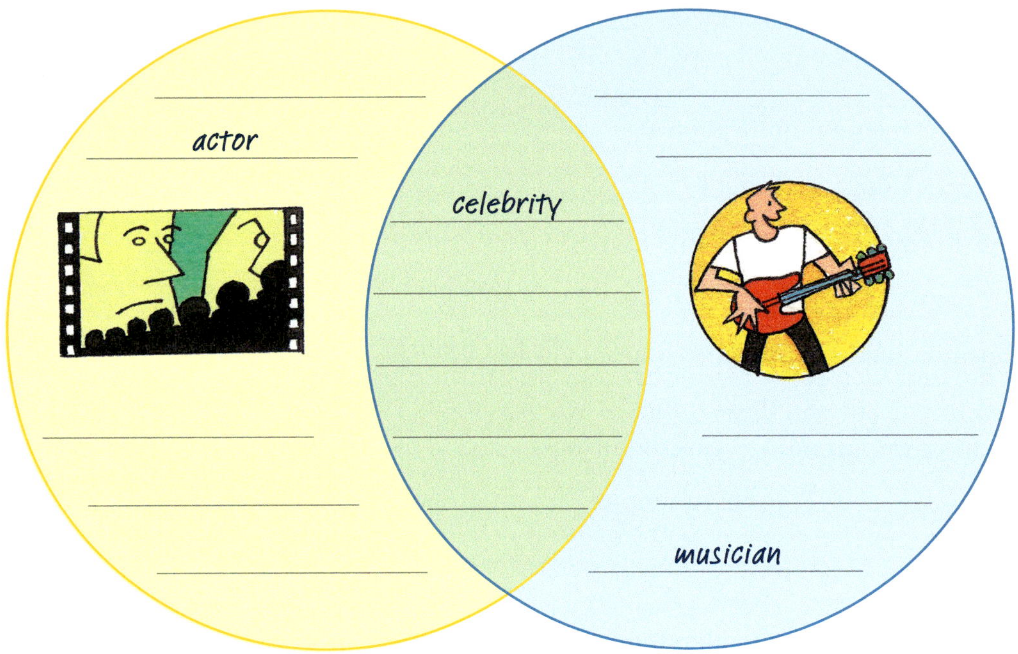

2 Film reviews

Complete the extracts from film reviews with these adjectives.

action-packed! · funny! · scary! · romantic! · thrilling! · amazing! · silly!

Example: It's a very *funny* comedy – the best I've seen this year.

1 It's a ______________ film about two young lovers.

2 The plot was so __________, it was completely unbelievable.

3 This horror film is really __________ – prepare for a fright!

4 The special effects were _____________ : it surprised me how good they were.

5 It was a really _____________ drama. I didn't know how it was going to end.

6 The film is __________________ from start to finish. There are fights, car crashes and disasters ...

Working with language

3 -ing form or infinitive?

Write each verb in the correct column. Some verbs may belong in both columns.

~~admit~~ • agree • choose • continue • decide • hate • hope • learn • like • love • start • stop • suggest • would like

+ ing form	+ infinitive	+ ing form	+ infinitive
admit			

4 Cartoon captions

Complete the captions using the phrases in the box in the correct form.

become a rock star • break the window • ~~play American football~~ • play the guitar • talk • watch football

Example: Harry hated *playing / to play American football.*

1  Laura would like ____________________.

2 Hamid never stops __________.

3  Meera loves ____________________.

4 Emma is learning ____________________.

5  Jamie admitted ____________________.

5 Maria Sharapova

Complete with the -ing form or infinitive of the verbs in brackets. Both forms may be possible.

Maria Sharapova was born in Nyagan, Russia. From the age of four she loved *playing / to play* [1] (play) tennis. When she was six, trainers said that she had a chance of ____________ [2] (become) a professional tennis player. Ex-tennis star Martina Navratilova suggested ____________ [3] (take) Maria to the USA, and Maria's parents decided ____________ [4] (follow) Martina's advice. At the age of nine, Maria started ____________ [5] (train) at the famous Bollettieri Sports Academy in Florida.

In 2001, at the age of 14, Maria's dream of ____________ [6] (play) tennis as a professional became reality. Over the next three years she continued ____________ [7] (get) stronger and faster.

In 2004 Maria won Wimbledon by ____________ [8] (beat) Serena Williams 6–1, 6–4. She was only 17 years old. At the age of 18 she was already the world's highest paid female athlete.

Revision

6 Short answers

Foxtel magazine is interviewing actor and rapper Will Smith. Write short answers to complete Will's answers.

Foxtel: Are you working on a new movie at the moment?

Will: *No, I'm not.* [1] I'm recording a rap album.

Foxtel: Were your parents in showbiz?

Will: ____________ [2] My mom worked in a school and my pop repaired fridges.

Foxtel: When you made your first album, did you expect to be famous?

Will: ____________ [3] When I first heard my music on the radio, I knew anything was possible.

Foxtel: Are you going to continue making music?

Will: ____________ [4] I will always continue to rap.

Foxtel: When you got your first TV role, did you find acting easy?

Will: ____________ [5] At first I was a terrible actor!

Foxtel: Have you ever made a bad career choice?

Will: ____________ [6] I said 'No thanks' to Keanu Reeve's role in *The Matrix*, for example.

Abridged and adapted from: http://www.jazzyjefffreshprince.com/interviews/will-smith/will-smith-hitch-a-star.htm

Writing

7 My favourite film

Make notes about your favourite film. Then write a review (100–120 words).

What is the film called?	
Who stars in it?	
What kind of film is it?	drama ☐, comedy ☐, love story ☐, action film ☐, cartoon ☐, horror film ☐, other:
What is it about?	
What happens?	
Why do you like it?	

My favourite film is called

Ich kann ...

Complete the table with things you can do in English.

sagen, was ich gerne mache:	*I like*
meine Interessen ausdrücken:	*I'm*
eine Entscheidung mitteilen:	*I've decided*
eine Überlegung äußern:	*I'm thinking of*
eine Erinnerung an etwas, was ich gemacht habe, ausdrücken:	*I remember* *that film.*
jemanden nach seinen/ihren Zukunftsplänen fragen:	*What do you hope*
einen Dank erwidern:	

12 How others live

Working with words

1 Crossword

Complete the crossword. The number of letters is shown in brackets.

1 Au-pair-Mädchen/Junge (2 + 4)
2 Kost und Logis (5 + 3 + 7)
3 Arbeiter/in auf einem Bauernhof (4 + 6)
4 Visum (4)
5 Nachtleben (9)
6 freiwillig (9)
7 Umweltschutz (12)
8 behandeln (5)
9 Urlaubsort (7 + 6)

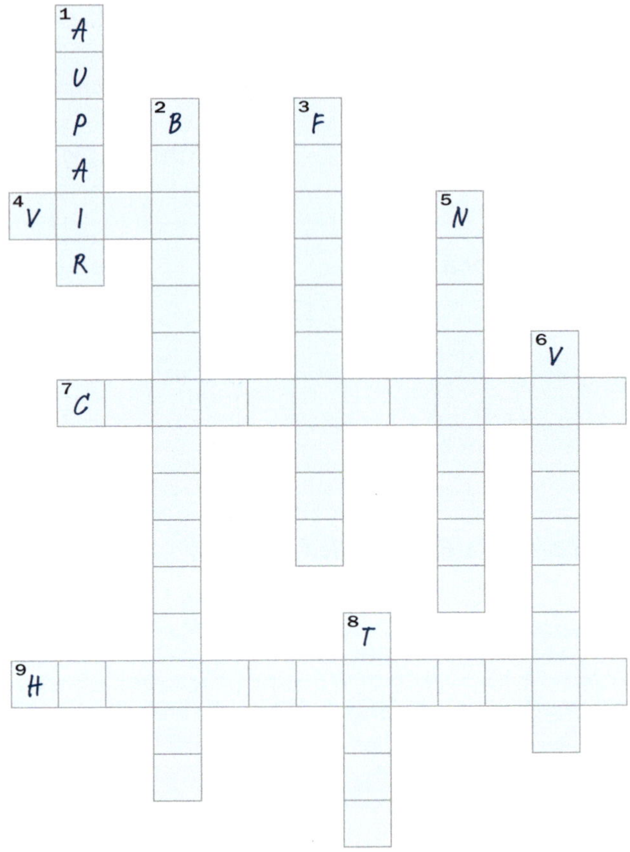

2 Working holidays

Complete the speech bubbles with the words from the crossword.

I'm working as a ____________ [1] volunteer in South Africa. Because it's ____________ [2] work, I don't need a working ________ [3].

I'm working in Texas as a ____________ [6]. The money isn't great, but I get free ____________ ____________ [7].

It's fun working at a ____________ [4] in Australia. The tourists are friendly and the ____________ [5] is great!

I'm really enjoying my job in London as an ____________ [8]. The kids are nice and they ________ [9] me like one of the family.

Working with language

3 The passive

Complete the table with the passive forms of the verb to pay. Some of the parts are given.

Aussagen	Verneinungen	Fragen	Kurzantworten
simple present			
I *am paid*.	I ______.	______ I ______?	Yes, I ______. No, I ______.
She ______.	She *isn't paid*.	______ she ______?	Yes, she ______. No, she ______.
They ______.	They ______.	*Are* they *paid*?	Yes, they ______. No, they ______.
present perfect			
He ______.	He ______.	______ he ______?	Yes, he ______. No, he ______.
We ______.	We ______.	______ we ______?	Yes, we ______. No, we ______.
simple past			
I ______.	I ______.	______ I ______?	Yes, I ______. No, I ______.
You ______.	You ______.	______ you ______?	Yes, you ______. No, you ______.
will future			
We ______.	We ______.	______ we ______?	Yes, we ______. No, we ______.

4 Passive sentences

Complete the English sentences.

Example: Die Tiere werden täglich gefüttert. (feed) The animals *are fed every day*.

1 Mein Pass wurde gestern gestohlen. (steal) My passport ______.

2 Das Auto ist noch nicht repariert worden. (repair) The car ______.

3 Wird in Singapur Englisch gesprochen? (speak) ______ in Singapore?

4 Hat man dir letztes Jahr ein eigenes Schlafzimmer gegeben? (give)

______ your own bedroom last year?

5 Ihre Unterkunft wird nicht von der Firma gestellt werden. (provide)

Your accommodation ______.

6 Nächstes Jahr werden mehr Freiwillige gebraucht. (need)

More volunteers ______ next year.

5 Travel advice

Complete with the correct passive forms of the verbs in brackets. Be careful with the tenses.

Stay safe in Aussie

Australia *is visited*[1] (visit) by over 5 million tourists every year – 140,000 of them from Germany. It's a friendly, laid-back country – but it can be very dangerous for tourists. Almost 400 tourists ______________[2] (kill) last year in Australia. Here are some tips to stay safe:

- In northern Australia, several tourists ______________[3] (eat) by crocodiles in recent years. If you ______________[4] (warn) about crocodiles in the water, don't swim!
- If your car stops in the Outback, you ______________[5] (find) faster if you stay with the car.
- The Australian countryside is very dry: many serious fires ______________[6] (start) in recent years by careless visitors, so be careful with cigarettes, etc.
- If you see a snake, stay calm and move away slowly. Snakes are not normally aggressive if they ______________[7] (leave) alone.
- Kangaroos look friendly, but they are big animals and can be dangerous. If they ______________[8] (feed) by tourists, they can become too friendly!

Revision

6 Adverbs of manner

a Write the adverbs which go with these adjectives.

careful	*carefully*	good	______
easy	______	nice	______
fast	______	noisy	______

b Say how (not) to do these things, using the adverbs from the table.

Example: You have to fill in this form *carefully* – it's easy to make a mistake.

1 Quiet! The koalas will run away if you walk ______________.
2 If you do the job ______________, you can stay for another month.
3 We will ______________ finish this job today – it won't take long.
4 Please speak to the guests ______________ – don't be rude to them!
5 Don't drive so ______________! This is a really bad road.

Writing

7 An interesting holiday

Write an article for a college magazine about an interesting place that you have visited. Write about 120 words. Start by making notes. Use your dictionary if necessary.

Name of place/country	
Sort of place	village ☐ small town ☐ city ☐ other:
Area	in the country ☐ in the mountains ☐ by the sea / a lake ☐ other:
Description of area and weather	
Accommodation	
When did you go there?	
The people	
The language (if relevant)	
Food and drink	
Things to do	
Your general impressions	

Ich kann ...

Complete the table with things you can do in English.

nach Unterschieden zwischen zwei Dingen fragen:	*What's the*
sagen, was man in einem anderen Land machen kann:	*In Australia, you can*
sagen, dass ich etwas ganz okay finde:	*It's* … *suppose.*
unpersönlich Fakten beschreiben:	*My mobile phone has been* *The fence will*

13 Modern love

Working with words

1 Definitions

Complete the definitions. The first letter of each word has been given.

1 If you have a child but you don't have a partner, you are a *s* ______ *p* ______.
2 A person who looks after children for the parents is called a *c* ______.
3 A woman who is going to have a baby is *p* ______.
4 A person who does what he/she wants is *i* ______.
5 When a man and a woman want to become husband and wife they *g* ______ *m* ______.
6 If you look after a child until it grows up, you *b* ______ it *u* ______.

2 All about relationships

a Use the prepositions in the box to complete the expressions.

about • for • from • on • to • up • with • with

1 to be angry ______ someone
2 to make life difficult ______ someone
3 to ban someone ______ somewhere
4 to be worried ______ something/someone
5 to count ______ someone
6 to split ______ ______ someone
7 to be nice ______ someone

b Help Anja to complete her email to her British penfriend, using expressions from part a.

Hi Jill,

How are you? I'm okay, but I'm *worried about* 1 (sich Sorgen machen um) my sister, Dani. Her boyfriend is continuing to ______ 2 (jdm das Leben schwer machen) her, but she doesn't want to ______ 3 (Schluss machen mit) him. He sees other girls and he steals money from her – and me. I would like to ______ 4 (ihm den Zutritt verweigern) my flat, but then Dani will ______ 5 (wütend sein auf) me. She says that I should ______ 6 (nett sein zu) him. She knows that she can ______ 7 (sich verlassen auf) me because I'm her sister, but I think that this boy is ruining her life.

Any ideas?

love, Anja

Working with language

3 The past perfect

Complete the sentences with the past perfect of the verbs in brackets.

Example: Rob felt ill because he *had drunk* (drink) too much beer the night before.

1 Ben felt much happier after Sarah ________________ (call) him.

2 When we got to the bus stop, the bus ______________________ (already leave) .

3 Leah lost her job because she _______________ (be) late for work every day that week.

4 After she __________________ (split up) with Andy, Beth started to go out with Tim.

5 I missed your call because I _______________ (go) out.

6 Dan's phone stopped working after he ___________________ (drop) it in the swimming pool.

4 Indirect speech

Complete the table.

Direkte Rede	Indirekte Rede
simple present 'I'm sorry!'	*simple past* *She said that she was sorry.*
simple past 'I saw Jill in town.'	*past perfect* *She said* ________________
present perfect 'Tom has lost his keys.'	________________ *She said that Tom had lost his keys.*
will 'I'll see you later.'	*would* ________________
can 'You can use my phone.'	________________ ________________

'She said she was too ill to come to school today!'

5 Classroom gossip

Report what they said.

Example: Anthony said that *Brad had asked Alison for a date.*

1 Tom said that ______________________________

2 Emma ______________________________

3 Louise ______________________________

4 Jackie ______________________________

5 Brad ______________________________

6 He ______________________________

Revision

6 Conditional 1

Use the words in brackets to translate the sentences into English.

Example: Wenn sie schwanger wird, werden ihre Eltern sauer. (get pregnant / take it badly)

If she gets pregnant, her parents will take it badly.

1 Rob wird traurig sein, wenn Alice einen neuen Freund findet. (be sad / get a new boyfriend)

____

2 Wenn du nicht vorsichtig fährst, machst du einen Unfall. (drive carefully / have an accident)

____

3 Wenn er nicht rechtzeitig zum Vorstellungsgespräch kommt, wird er die Stelle nicht bekommen. (be late for / not get the job)

____

4 Wenn es regnet, wird die Grillparty eine Katastrophe. (rain / be a disaster)

____

Writing

7 Problems, problems

a Dan writes to an internet forum about his 'girlfriend problem'. Read his message, then answer the questions with your own opinions.

I've met a girl and I really like her. Her name is Carol and she goes to the same karate class as me. I think she likes me too, but I'm not sure.
We went out two weeks ago, and afterwards she said that she had had a great time. She also said that she would go out with me again. Since then I have tried to call her, but she never answers her phone, and she hasn't replied to my text messages. She hasn't been to karate either. I know that she is having problems at home with her stepdad.
What should I do? I don't want to seem too keen, but I don't want to lose her.

Dan

1 Does Carol like Dan, in your opinion? ______
2 Does she want to go out with him again? ______
3 Why hasn't she called him? ______
4 Is she really having problems at home? ______
5 What should Dan do? ______
6 Why should he do this? ______

b Write a message to the forum, using your answers to part a.

Hi Dan,

______

______

______

______

______

Ich kann ...

Complete the table with things you can do in English.

erzählen, warum etwas in der Vergangenheit geschehen ist:	*My mother was angry with me because I* ______
berichten, was jemand gesagt oder gefragt hat:	*Jimmy told me that he* ______ *I asked her* ______
Zahlen in einer Tabelle beschreiben:	*More than twenty* ______

14 Kicking the habit

Working with words

1 Bad habits

Join words from A and B to make eight phrases to do with smoking, drugs and alcohol. Write the German meaning next to each phrase.

A

					D	E					
				R	J	K	B				
			S	T	O	P	H	A			
		V	B	L	T	G	E	I	D		
	E	D	Q	A	Z	X	A	G	O	X	
S	Q	Y	C	X	B	P	L	J	E	P	A
C	I	G	A	R	E	T	T	E	X	T	X
	S	X	W	X	C	P	H	U	G	A	
		N	K	N	O	A	L	J	H		
			I	M	M	N	Y	E			
				F	E	I	K				
					F	C					

B

ATTACKDRUNKGLUEREACTIONSWOKESMOKINGUNCONSCIOUSWARNING

sniff glue – Klebstoff schnüffeln

____

____

____

____

____

____

____

2 Advertising campaign

Complete each advertising message with the best verbs from the box.

deny • depend on (x 2) • ~~enjoy~~ • give up • hurt • persuade • refuse • shorten

1 *Enjoy* life – ______ smoking.

2 You ______ to see the risks. Every cigarette ______ your life by 11 minutes.

3 How can your child ______ you if you ______ drugs?
Get help with your drug problem before you ______ the ones you love.

4 'Before the accident, I thought nothing could ______ me to stop drinking and driving.'
Don't ______ the danger – alcohol and driving don't mix.

Working with language

3 Conditional II and III

Complete the table.

	Bedingung	Folge
Typ II	*simple past* If he ______ (stop) smoking,	*would + Infinitiv* he ______ (be) healthier.
Typ III	*past perfect* If he ______ (stop) smoking,	______ *Partizip Perfekt* he ______ (be) healthier.

4 Conditional sentences

Cross out the incorrect verb forms.

Example: Ruby would get better grades if she *worked* / ~~*would work*~~ harder.

1 If I *didn't go* / *wouldn't go* to parties, I would have a boring life.
2 If you had come to my party, you *would have* / *would have had* a great time.
3 Dan would be fitter if he *doesn't eat* / *didn't eat* junk food.
4 I would have gone out with Susie if she *had phoned* / *would have phoned* me.
5 He wouldn't have lost his job if he *hadn't been* / *wasn't* late for work.
6 Alice and Mick wouldn't argue if they *drank* / *would drink* less.

5 'If I stopped smoking ...' (Conditional II)

Jack always has an answer. Help him to explain why he won't stop smoking.

Dad: 'If you stopped smoking, you would be healthier.'
Jack: 'Yes, but ...

1 If I ______ (stop) smoking, I ______ (have) more money.
2 If I ______ (have) more money, I ______ (go) out more.
3 If I ______ (go) out more, I ______ (have) less time for school work.
4 If I ______ (have) less time for school work, I ______ (not pass) my exams.
5 If I ______ pass (not pass) my exams, I ______ (not get) a good job.

So I'm not going to stop smoking!'

6 If things had been different … (Conditional III)

Alvin Parsley was a great rock star 20 years ago, but now he's dead. His friends and fans are talking about what he should have done differently. Find the best ending for each sentence and put the verbs into the correct form.

~~be healthier~~ • not become so fat • go to the gym more often • live a healthy life • not have a heart attack • not spend all his money • spend more time at home

Example: "If Alvin had given up smoking, he *would have been healthier*."

1 "He would have been fitter if he ______."

2 "He would have been rich if he ______."

3 "His wife wouldn't have split up with him if he ______."

4 "If he had eaten less junk food, he ______."

5 "If he had drunk less, he ______."

6 "Maybe, but his music would have been boring if he ______."

Revision

7 The passive

Translate the sentences into English, using the words in brackets.

Example: Die Warnhinweise werden von Rauchern nicht gelesen. (health warnings / read / smokers)

The health warnings aren't read by smokers.

1 Jedes Jahr werden 450 000 Deutsche bei Autounfällen verletzt.
(every year / Germans / hurt / car crashes)

______

2 Wird in diesem Club Ecstasy verkauft? (ecstasy / sell / nightclub)

______

3 Wurde der Unfall schon der Polizei gemeldet? (the accident / report / to the police / yet)

______

4 Letztes Jahr wurden auf dem Oktoberfest 4 Millionen Liter Bier getrunken.
(last year / 6 million litres of beer / drink / at the Oktoberfest)

______

5 Mir ist gestern Abend in der Kneipe mein ganzes Geld gestohlen worden.
(all my money / steal / in the pub / last night)

______

6 Wie viele Jugendliche werden nächstes Jahr durch Drogen ums Leben kommen?
(young people / kill / drugs / next year)

______

Writing

8 Lifestyle advice

a Read about Sarah, then put the phrases from the box next to the correct heading in the list.

Sarah is 18. She is quite fit and goes swimming every day, and she doesn't eat junk food. Sarah smokes about 10 cigarettes a day. She started smoking when she was 14. She has tried to give up, but she says that it is 'too hard'. She doesn't often drink alcohol, but when she goes to a party (about once a month), she drinks a lot of vodka. She also sometimes has an ecstasy tablet when she is out clubbing with her friends, but she says that ecstasy is 'just a soft drug'.

bad for your heart and lungs • bad reaction • become unconscious • cut down • ~~do regular exercise~~ • eat healthily • get drunk • get in trouble with the police • panic attack • soft drinks • stop!

good habits: *do regular exercise,* ______

effect of smoking on health: ______

effects of alcohol and drugs: ______

______

advice: ______

b Now use the list to write your opinion on Sarah's lifestyle (about 120 words):

Sarah's lifestyle is ______

______

______

______

______

______

______

______

Ich kann ...

Complete the table with things you can do in English.

eine unwahrscheinliche Bedingung formulieren:	*If I smoked, I* ______
fragen, was jemand in einer bestimmten Situation machen würde:	*What would you do if* ______
jemanden etwas empfehlen:	*If I were you,* ______
sagen, was geschehen wäre, wenn ...:	*If we had left home earlier,* ______

15 Drive to arrive alive ...

Working with words

1 Warning!

Complete the text and the crossword. The words are the same. (Hint: use the crossword to find out how many letters there are in each word.)

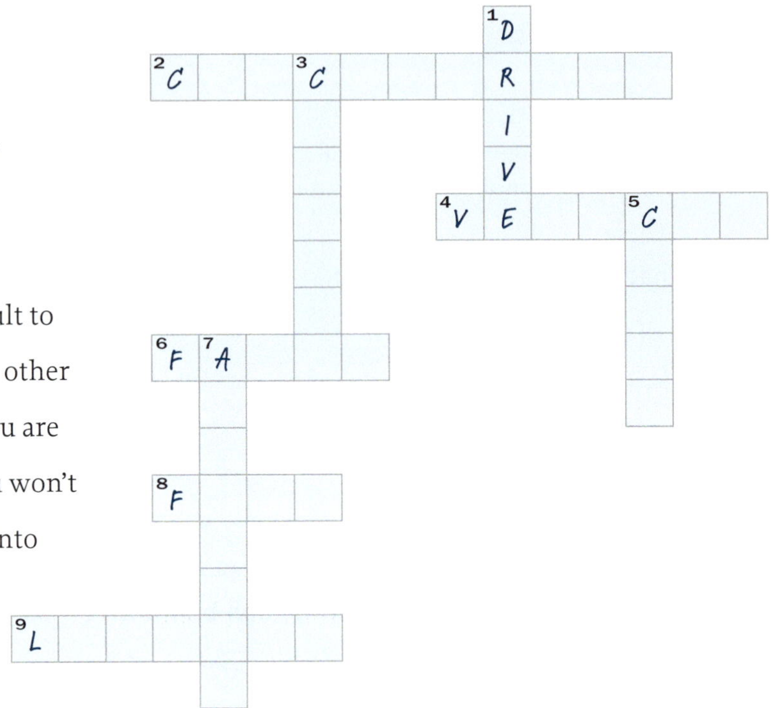

Don't phone and *drive* **1.**

If you are talking on the phone, it's difficult to ________ 2 on the road and the other traffic around you. You may think that you are in ________ 3 of your car, but you won't be able to stop quickly and you may run into another ________ 4 or a pedestrian.

You may have to go to ________ 5 if it is your ________ 6.

Even if you don't cause an ________ 7, the police can stop you and make you pay a ________ 8.

You could even lose your ________ 9.

2 Cars

Tom has some problems with his car. Match the letters in the picture to the sentences below. Use a dictionary if necessary.

1 [*a*] I have a flat tyre.
2 [ ] The windscreen is broken.
3 [ ] There's an oil leak.
4 [ ] The boot won't shut.
5 [ ] The engine isn't running properly.
6 [ ] The headlights don't work.
7 [ ] I've run out of petrol.

Working with language

3 The past progressive

Complete the table with forms of the verb to read. Some of the parts have been done for you.

Aussagen	Verneinungen	Fragen	Kurzantworten
I *was reading*.	I ______ .	______ I ______ ?	Yes, *I was*. No, I ______ .
You ______ .	You ______ .	______ you ______ ?	Yes, you ______ . No, you ______ .
She ______ .	She *wasn't reading*.	*Was* she *reading*?	Yes, she ______ . No, she ______ .
We ______ .	We ______ .	______ we ______ ?	Yes, we ______ . No, we *weren't*.
They ______ .	They ______ .	______ they ______ ?	Yes, they ______ . No, they ______ .

4 Party gossip

Your friend went to a party last night. He took some photos with his mobile, but you can't see all the details. You want to know what was happening. Ask questions in the past progressive.

Example: why / Anna / look sad ? *Why was Anna looking sad?*

1 who / dance / with Anja? ______

2 what / Alex / drink? ______

3 Ralf / chat up / Sandra? ______

4 why / Silke and Joe / laugh? ______

5 'No, I wasn't!'

Mrs Jones is a very strict teacher. Help the class to make excuses.

Example: Sally! You were sleeping! (think about German verbs)

I wasn't sleeping. I was thinking about German verbs.

1 Rob! You were sending a text message! (browse a web page)

______

2 Tim and Liam! You were fighting in the break! (practise judo)

______

3 Jed and Ben! You were chatting! (discuss our answers)

______

4 Hollie! You were copying Phil's answers! (help him with his work)

______

6 while or during?

Cross out the wrong word in each sentence.

1 My boyfriend always rings ~~*during*~~ / *while* my favourite soap is on.
2 Sandy fell asleep *during* / *while* she was doing her homework.
3 He sent a text message *during* / *while* the lesson.
4 We saw Richard and Lucy *during* / *while* we were cruising around town.
5 Please switch off your mobile phones *during* / *while* the film.

7 Relative clauses

Translate the sentences into German. Always use a relative pronoun.

1 The boys drinking beer got into trouble.

____

2 The girl standing at the traffic lights is my sister.

____

3 Didn't you see the old lady crossing the road?

____

4 The person driving the car wasn't injured.

____

5 Who was that boy smoking in the toilets?

____

6 The woman talking loudly on the phone was really annoying me.

____

Revision

8 Indirect speech

Put the conversation into indirect speech.

Cyclist: You're an idiot! (1) You nearly hit me!
Motorist: (2) You're talking rubbish. (3) You just fell off your bike.
Cyclist: (4) You'll kill someone if you drive like that.
Motorist: (5) You need a kid's bike with two extra wheels, then you won't fall off.

Example: *The cyclist said that the motorist was an idiot.*

1 *He said that she had* _______________
2 _______________
3 _______________
4 _______________
5 _______________

Writing

9 A funny thing happened ...

Write about a strange, an interesting or a funny thing that happened to you (or someone you know). Write about 120 words.

Start by making notes. Use a dictionary as necessary.

When did it happen?	
Where were you when it happened?	
What were you doing when it happened?	
What happened?	
What did you do/say?	
What did other people do/say?	
How did you feel?	
How did it end?	

Ich kann ...

Complete the table with things you can do in English.

mich im Gruppengespräch zu Wort melden:	*Can I just*
jemanden anderen ins Gespräch einbringen:	*What do*
höflich widersprechen:	*You may be*
erzählen, was in der Vergangenheit geschah, während eine andere Handlung ablief:	*When we arrived,*
	I was having a shower when
eine Autofahrt beschreiben:	*I was driving along when I came to*
	Another car

Quellenverzeichnis

FOTOS:

Titel: Corbis/G. Steiner; Visum/G. Schönharting; Caro/Oberhäuser
Corbis: S. 9/1/Star; S. 9/4/5/7RF; S. 19/B. Krist; S. 24/RF/WV; S. 38/M. Prince; S. 40/RF/WV; S. 48/1/R. Schultheiss; S. 48/2/Creasource; S. 48/3/E. Klawitter; S. 48/4/R. Holz; S. 61/L. Manning;
Fotofinder: S. 9/3/Alimidi.net/C. Prandl; S. 27/Visum/G. Schlaeger; S. 34/Photothek; S. 50/NPL/Arco Digital Images; S. 40/plus49/J. Becker
Getty Images: S. 9/2/RF; S. 9/6/P. Correz; S. 9/8/V. Besmault; S. 40/RF;
David Graham: S. 5/WV
V. Maly: S. 32/1/2;
Picture Alliance: S. 36/EPA/P. Hilton; S. 39/Zentralbild/G. Mauricio; S. 40/S. Montgomery; S. 46/1/A. Khayat; S. 46/2/dpa/S. Wöstmann; S. 57/dpa/F. Leonhardt
Stockfood: S. 23/Eising